Dance Is Fun!

by Robin Nelson

first step nonfiction

⌐Lerner Publications Company · Minneapolis

LERNER

SOURCE™

Expand learning beyond the printed book. Download free, complementary educational resources for this book from our website, www.lerneresource.com.

The images in this book are used with the permission of: © Cusp/SuperStock, p. 4; © iStockphoto.com/ Christopher Futcher, p. 5; © iStockphoto.com/Carmen Martínez Banús, p. 6; © Flirt/SuperStock, pp. 7, 8; © Ruth Jenkinson/Dorling Kindersley/Getty Images, p. 9; © iStockphoto.com/Summer Derrick, p 10; © iStockphoto.com/Spiderplay, p. 11; © Paha_L/Bigstock.com, pp. 12, 17; © sarah beard buckley/Flickr/Getty Images, p. 13; © iStockphoto.com/Donna Coleman, p. 14; © iStockphoto.com/ Jeffrey Zavitski, p. 15; © palbl4/Bigstock.com, p. 16; © Alistair Berg/The Image Bank/Getty Images, p. 18; © Marco Del Grande/The Sydney Morning Herald/Fairfax Media/Getty Images, p. 19; © Laura Westlund/Independent Picture Service, p. 21.

Front cover: © Hybrid Images/Cultura/Getty Images.

Main body text set in ITC Avant Garde Gothic Std Medium 21/25.
Typeface provided by Adobe Systems.

Lerner Publications Company
A division of Lerner Publishing Group, Inc.
241 First Avenue North
Minneapolis, MN 55401 U.S.A.

Website address: www.lernerbooks.com

Library of Congress Cataloging-in-Publication Data

Nelson, Robin, 1971–
    Dance is fun! / by Robin Nelson.
        pages   cm — (First step nonfiction - Sports are fun!)
    Includes index.
    ISBN 978–1–4677–1104–3 (lib. bdg. : alk. paper)
    ISBN 978–1–4677–1745–8 (eBook)
    1. Dance—Juvenile literature. I. Title.
GV1596.5.N45 2014
792.8—dc23   2012046922

Manufactured in the United States of America
1 – PC – 7/15/13

Table of Contents

Dance

Do you like to move your body to music?

You can dance!

Ballet

Ballet tells stories with dance.

Ballet dancers wear ballet shoes.

Ballet begins with five **positions**.

Ballet dancers leap and twirl.

Tap

Tap dancers make noise with their shoes.

Tap shoes have metal on them.

Tap dancers tap their toes.

Tap dancers **shuffle** their feet.

Jazz

Jazz dancing is fun.

Jazz dancers move to fast music.

Sometimes they dance in plays or other shows.

Jazz dancers have lots of energy.

Let's Dance!

You can dance alone or with friends.

There are so many ways to dance!

A Dance Studio

A dance studio is where dancers practice. There are giant mirrors on the wall. A ballet studio has a **barre**. Dancers hold onto the barre when they are warming up.

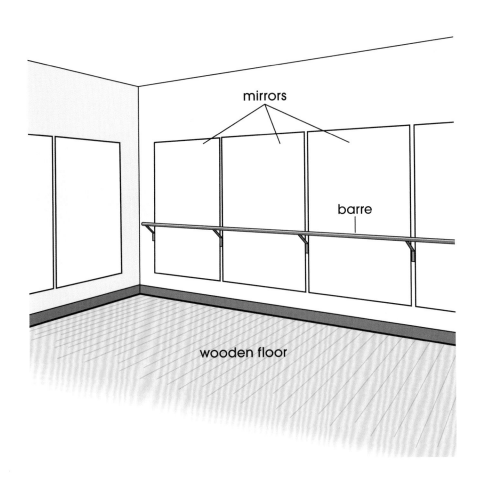

mirrors

barre

wooden floor

21

Fun Facts

- It is important to warm up before dancing so you don't get hurt.

- Dancers dance on a stage in a dance recital. They wear costumes too.

- Dancing is great exercise! It uses lots of muscles and gets your heart pumping.

Glossary

ballet – a kind of dancing that uses dance and music to tell a story

barre – a wooden bar that is attached to a wall in a ballet studio

jazz – a kind of dancing with rhythm where dancers make up their own moves

positions – one of five ways in which ballet dancers move their feet. These five positions are the basis for all ballet steps.

shuffle – to slide your feet back and forth on the ground

Index